Rock-pooling

Written by Emma Lynch

This is the coast.

We are going rock-pooling.

This is a rock pool.

The rock pool is deep.
Look at the floating weeds.

net

This is a shrimp net.

Look at this shrimp.
Shrimps are not big.

This is a crab.
Crabs are shellfish.

Look at the fish.
They are swimming.

This is a sailing boat.

sail

See it float along.

Gulls sit high up on the rocks.

They swoop to get the food.

Wet shells look bright in the sun.

It is night at the coast.
The rock pool is still.

boat

crab

fish

gull

shells

shrimp

Things we can see at the coast